Roderick A. Williams
6184 Floral Lakes Drive
Delray Beach, FL 33484
561-316-8919 Cell 561-637-6586 Home
Willriams@gmail.com

about 5000 words

P.O.E.M.S.

Poetry Of Egoistical Manic Schizophrenic

P.O.E.M.S. Vol. 1
PTSD EGOTISTICAL MANIC SCHIZOPHRENIC
BY RODERICK A. WILLIAMS SR.

P.O.E.M.S.

VOL. 1

PTSD OF EGOTISTICAL MANIC SCHIZOPHRENIC

BY

RODERICK A. WILLIAMS

PREFACE

THE VOICE STARTED ABOUT DECEMBER OF 2014. THEY ONLY BEGAN TO GET LOUDER. I STARTED WRITING POETRY WHEN I WAS ABOUT 13· IT WAS AN OUTLET FOR ME TO EXPRESS MYSELF WHEN THINGS IN HOUSEHOLD WERE UNBEARABLE. FATHER WAS A BLUE-COLLAR WORKER BORN DURING BABY BOOMERS, ALCOHOL WAS HIS FORM OF RELAXATION. DRUG ABUSE THROUGHOUT HIS TEENAGE YEARS TIL ABOUT THE TIME HE DIED. MY MOTHER BORN DURING THE 60'S… DRUG COCKTAIL OF STORIES HERE AS WELL. GREAT GRANDFATHER HIRED ASSASSIN IN TWO PUBLISHED BOOKS, "CANARY THAT SANG, BUT COULDN'T FLY, & MURDER INCORPORATED." THAT STORY MAYBE FOR LATER DATE!!! ABOUT 2007 MY FATHER WAS DIAGNOSED SCHIZOPHRENIC BI-POLAR, HIS DRINKING WORSE. RAGES OF FURY AFTER A DAY & NIGHT BENIGN. SOME OF THESE POEMS RELATE TO THOSE MOMENTS WITH BOTH MY PARENTS IN. ABOUT THE END 2014 THE VOICES STARTED. ABOUT SIX MONTHS AFTER MY GRANDFATHER ON THE MAIDEN SIDE PASSED AWAY. THE VOICES BEGIN TO GET LOUDER. SOMETIMES THEY CONSUME ME. I'M ABLE TO FIGHT THEM!!! THESE POEMS ARE SOME OF THOSE RESULTS. HERITAGE OF "SCHIZOPHRENIC IS A SEVERE PSYCHOTIC DISORDER THAT AFFECTS ABOUT 1 PERCENT OF THE POPULATION HAVING AN FDR SUCH AS

A PARENT OR SIBLING WITH SCHIZOPHRENIA INCREASES THE RISK TO 10 PERCENT,"
ACCORDING TO <u>NATIONAL ALLIANCE ON MENTAL ILLNESS (NAMI</u>)& AN ARTICLE IN USA
TODAY, 2018. "RISK JUMPS TO 50 PERCENT IF BOTH PARENTS HAVE BEEN DIAGNOSED,

"**THE ENVIRONMENT.** BEING EXPOSED TO VIRUSES OR TOXINS, OR EXPERIENCING
MALNUTRITION BEFORE BIRTH, CAN INCREASE THE RISK OF SCHIZOPHRENIA.

- **BRAIN CHEMISTRY.** ISSUES WITH BRAIN CHEMICALS, SUCH AS THE
NEUROTRANSMITTERS DOPAMINE AND GLUTAMATE, MAY CONTRIBUTE TO
SCHIZOPHRENIA.

- **SUBSTANCE USE.** TEEN AND YOUNG ADULT USE OF MIND-ALTERING (PSYCHOACTIVE
OR PSYCHOTROPIC) DRUGS MAY INCREASE THE RISK OF SCHIZOPHRENIA.

- **IMMUNE SYSTEM ACTIVATION.** SCHIZOPHRENIA CAN ALSO BE CONNECTED
TO AUTOIMMUNE DISEASES OR INFLAMMATION.

ALL ACCORDING TO AN ARTICLE ON HEALTH LINE 2021

THE GENETICS HOME REFERENCE INDICATES, THAT MOST PEOPLE WITH A CLOSE RELATIVE
WITH SCHIZOPHRENIA WILL NOT DEVELOP THE DISORDER THEMSELVES."

SOME THESE POEMS ARE RESULTS OF A DRUG INFUSED SELF-MEDICATING & LEGALLY
MEDICATING EMOTIONS, AT TIMES I HEAR THINGS BEFORE THE HAPPEN, MONTHS BEFORE,
DAY, MINUTES, DATELINE NEWS, VIOLENCE LIVE NOW ON THE TV SCREEN A ¼ OF A DAY OR
MORE BEFORE IT HAPPEN... OTHER TIMES NOTHING

BUT A BOOK, AN OLD VOICE IN THE WIND, ALTHOUGH IN THE NEXT LIFE, OR A MEMORY, MY ENVISION OF DIFFERENT SCENES OR DESCRIPTION. A RANGE OF POEMS FROM 13 TO 36 OF AGE. SECLUSION FROM SOCIETY. DEPRESSION! CHILD ABUSE! EVEN A LATE POEM FOR MY FATHER WHO PASSED ON 9/11. INTROVERT CONVERSATIONS ARE KNOWN OF, BUT WHEN SOMEONE SPEAKS AND IT'S A UNEXPLAINABLE. WHEN IT'S A 1000 MILES AWAY. ANOTHER HEMISPHERE, YOUR LOCKED UP FOR WORDS. AND TIMES THE VOICE IS YOUR OWN. YOU MAY ONLY WRITE THE FORM YOU LEARNED TO EXPRESS YOURSELF. SINCE MY TEENS IT'S BEEN POETRY, LITTLE LOVE MESSAGE, OR DIARY ENTERS IN COMPOSITION AS A DRAW, OR DOODLE. MINE. POETRY. SONGWRITING. QUOTES. SLOGANS. AND LATER BECOME AN AUTHOR. ONE OF MY GOALS, WRITING THIS BOOK OF POETRY. A LOT OF PEOPLE DON'T REALIZE THEIR ABILITY TO BE A VOICE IN YOUR HOBBIES, THINGS THAT INTEREST YOU. IF ITS YOUR PASSION FOR IT. WRITING POETRY, SONGWRITING, FREEWRITING HAPPENS TO BE ONE OF MINE!!! MUSICIANS ARE HITTING ALL TIME HIGHS IN STREAMING MUSIC. LEGACY BEING MADE.

RECORDS BEING BROKE. NOW POETS & SHORT STORIES WRITERS. NEXT LEGENDARY QUOTES. CENTURY FELT SLOGANS... JUST MUSICIANS IS NOT THE ONLY OUTLET FOR THESE FOUR AREAS. BUT A GREAT PLACE TO BLOCK OUT THE NOISE OR LET IT IN. I GREW UP IN POOR CONDITION FROM LACK OF PARENT GUARDSHIP. DOMESTIC MENTAL ABUSE, EMOTIONAL DISTRAUGHT, AGGRESSION, OPPRESSION, TO SELF-INFLICTED AGONY & HARM. ALTHOUGH SELF-REVIVING AND CO-DEPENDING. WRITING WELL.... BECAME!!!!

MY THERAPY!!! MY MEDICATION!!!

WELCOME

TO

PTSD OR EGOTISTICAL MANIC SCHIZOPHRENIC!!!

WHEN YOU READ THESE POEMS, PLEASE TAKE NOTICE OF SOME THE PHRASES.

PLACEMENT OF WORD OF CHOICE. TO CREATE A MUSE. PATTERNS MAY ASSIST IN THE

PSYCHE BEHAVIOR, AND/OR AN ARTICULATION. 'POETRY IS ART! ART IS POETRY!'

SPECIAL THANKS

FIRST, MY MOTHER WITHOUT HER

THERE WOULDN'T BE A TOMORROW ALL FOUR MY GRANDPARENTS

FOR RAISING ME ALTHOUGH AT TIMES WAS DIFFICULT

MY SIBLINGS, FAMILY, & MY FRIENDS

IN LOVE MEMORY

OF

MY FATHER, RODERICK W. P. GILBRIDE JR.

& MY THREE CHILDREN HOOD FRIENDS

GIT, ERIC GRIFFIN

JESSE BATISTA

106, CHRISTOPHER SWAGER

"Every person has their secret sorrows,

which the universe knows not; and often,

times we call a person cold; when they're only sad."

— **Henry Wadsworth Longfellow**

TABLE OF CONTENTS

Voices in My Head

VOICE OF LOVE

VOICE OF DRUGS

VOICE OF VIOLENCE

VOICE OF TORELENCE

VOICE OF JOY

VOICE OF PUBLIC

VOICE OF PRIVATE

VOICE OF OUTCRY

VOICE OF LABORS

VOICE OF FEAR

VOICE OF ANGRY

VOICE OF REASONING

VOICE OF RECONSIDERING

VOICE OF OTHERS

VOICE OF YOU

VOICE OF US

VOICE OF MYSELF

NON FEEL SAFE

PYRRHIC VICTORY

PYRRHIC VICTORY; FROM,

AN ARROGANT CONGREGATION,

PILOTING OPPOSITION SUPPRESSION,

RISKY APPRAISAL,

BY REGIMES; EVASION,

FROM, CHAOTIC FORMS,

OF TASTELESSLY, IRONIC,

FICTITIOUS, DILEMMAS,

BESTOWING & SCRUTINIZING

SOCIETIES COALITION,

FROM, FASCIST WILD PITCHES,

OUT OF BOUND ECONOMICS,

BI-PARTISAN PHILOSOPHY,

QUESTIONING THE CAUSE & EFFECT,

DEFYING THE LAWS OF UNITY....

A.D.D.I.C.I.T.I.O.N.S.

ACTUALLY,

DEVOTED,

DETERMINED,

INTEGRITY,

COMPASSIONATELY,

TAUGHT,

INTANGIBLE,

OPPRESSION,

NECESSARY,

SERENITY...

MY LOGO OF LOVE

ALWAYS MY UNO,

ALWAYS MY REVERSAL,

MY DRAW TWO; MY DRAW FOUR,

MY SKIP; MIGHTY MOUSE TRAP,

MY YAHTZEE, RUBIK'S CUBE,

MY GUESS WHO? MOTEL UPGRADE,

MY GET OUT JAIL FREE,

MY CHANCE OF INSANITY,

MY EGO, MY DOVE,

MY AMIGO, MY PLUG,

MY LOGO OF LOVE...

DEATH TIL APART

DIRECTIONS

ETERNAL

ANSWERS

TIMELESS

HEAVENS

THESIS

IN

LIFE

ABILITIES

PORTRAITS

ACTUALLY

REVEALING

THEORIES

5/5/1955 - 9/11/2020

POPS DRANK,

UNDER A TAB,

UNDER A TAP,

UNDER A CAP,

BROKEN ANKLE OVERLOADED,

FITS 12 STEPS,

RAGE UFC CAGE,

RUMBLE IN JUNGLE

MUHAMMAD & FOREMAN,

TIL THE GRAVE,

STUMBLE IN KITCHEN,

ANOTHER TASTE,

RATHER ESCAPE WITH GIBBY'S,

THEN HIS WEALTH...

ZERO VALUES

AEROSOLIZED TRANSMISSION,

REPOSITORY DROPLETS,

AIR PISTONS, EMISSIONS,

GLOBAL WARMING,

GLOBAL WARNING,

DRIVING UNDER INFLUENCE,

DRIVING WHILE IMPAIRED,

PILED HIGH AND DEEP,

AMERICAN STANDARD,

DEGREES' BOWELS,

UNDERGARMENTS IN A BUNCH,

WRETCHED WRECKING,

AROMA FOUL, ALIENATED,

ZERO VALUES, BLACK FLAGGED,

THROW IN THE TOWEL PARTIES...

DAT EXTRA

DAT SAUCE,

EXTRA GRIMY,

DAT RELISH,

EXTRA GOAD,

DAT TASTE,

EXTRA NASTY,

DAT BREED,

EXTRA RARE,

DAT MENTALITY,

EXTRA SAVAGE,

DAT HUNGER,

EXTRA THIRSTY,

DAT HUSTLE,

EXTRA URGENT,

DAT TIMING,

EXTRA FLAWLESS...

NO FREE SMILES

DUCKLETS RUNNING,

TEARS ROLLING,

SUCK IT UP BUDDY,

I'M SHEER WRONG,

NOTICE, NOTICE,

BOO-HOO NOTES LEFT,

HOMIE, FUCK YOU,

PREYING ON THE WEAK,

MY TEENAGERS FRIENDS,

LOST MOMS & DAD LAST WEEK,

NO FREE SMILES,

NO MCDONALD'S LOVE,

NO BIG & TASTY; SOUTHERN CHICKEN,

ALL I ASKED FOR,

TWO FOR THREE DOLLARS,

MCDOUBLE,

YUM, YUM, YUM...

WHY YOU?

WHY? WHY?

WHY YOU?

EYEBALLING ME!

IS IT BECAUSE, I'M FLAMBOYANT?

IS IT BECAUSE, THE FLASHY BLING?

WHY? WHY?

WHY YOU?

EYEBALLING ME!

ARE YOU DAZED? INCOHERENT?

ARE YOU AMAZED AT WHAT YOU SEE?

WHY? WHY?

WHY YOU?

EYEBALLING ME!

OR AM I?

EPCOT

HOSTILE IN THE POSTURE,

SWAG, ATTITUDE, DEMEANOR,

LOST IN SPACE, WILLIAM,

DARTH VADER ODYSSEY, LUKE,

LONGITUDE, LATITUDE, BALLERINA,

BLACK HOLE CAROUSEL,

RING AROUND A ROSE,

SLEEPING BEAUTY, CINDERELLA,

GOLDEN RULE OF THUMBELINA,

STADIUM ARENAS,

SPARTANS THREE HUNDREDTH,

PIERCING A SCALE, UNVEILING,

JAG, RANGER NORRIS,

MARSHALL LAW...

YOU KNOW WHEN

ITS BAD SITUATION,

WHEN YOUR LOVE,

IS MY TEMPTATION,

PASSION BODY ACHING,

COMPASSION SO SACRED,

CAPSULING, BENDING. & BREAKING,

I DO WHAT YOU ASK ME,

JUST BE PATIENCE,

YOU KNOW WHEN,

I AM BEING REAL,

YOU KNOW WHEN,

I AM BEING FAKE...

A MATCH MADE

STRUCK BY,

A MATCH MADE,

FOR HEAVEN & HELL,

FOR EARTH & SPACE,

A TENNIS SPA & BROTHEL,

15, 30, 45, LOVE,

MY PURSE ON FRONT,

YOURS SKINS ON BACK,

19TH HOLE EARLY BIRD,

BUY ONE, GET HALF,

TACKED FROM THE BILL,

FROM THE CHECK,

15, 20, 25, GRATUITY,

AND I ONLY HAD,

ICE WATER & BUTTER WITH BREAD.

OUR DETENTION ZOO

ALLEGATIONS BOUT,

MY ALLIGATORS CROCS,

DOCKS TWO MET,

D.O.C. DOC-U-MENTS,

YORK PEPPERMINTS,

ALIBI; REPOUR,

RETAINER RESOURCE,

PERTAINING TO THE COURTS,

YOUR HONOR, JUDGE,

LIENS FOR RESTITUTION,

I REST MY INSTITUTION,

RECESS CHAMBERS,

THIS INSTANT; YOU TWO,

GRITS, QUAKERS OATES,

THREE MEALS & A BED,

OUR DETENTION ZOO,

DEPARTMENT OF CORRECTION,

REVENUE & DEBT...

ROMANTIC TRANQUILITY

IS THIS A TURTLE? IS THIS A HARE?

IS THIS A RAT? IS IT A HORSE?

TRANQUILIZED TRANQUILITY,

CAT LOG: CATCH A GREAT WHITE,

WISDOM HIGHLIGHT; GREY WHITE,

AT THE DECIBELS MILLIONTHS SCALE,

DEMONS' REBELLION, ANGELS' ENVY,

QUE THE PAST; ELAPSE,

HIDE & SEEK, HIDIN' PEEPS,

GOD'S WRATH; DEVIL'S PRIDE,

DOG HASTING BURG GETTY'S BEEF,

AVALANCHE ARCTIC ARTIST,

ARSENAL ARTISTIC HARPS,

A ROMANTIC ETERNITY...

IS THIS A TURTLE? IS THIS A HARE?

IS THIS A RAT? IS IT A HORSE?

¼ OF CENTURY'S EVOKE

ARSE AGONY

REANGLING ASSES

IDENTIFY MASSES

STUDENTS GROUNDED

MASTER DOCTORATES FLOW

EXHAUSTING CARBURETOR

TRENDS BURNT'

GOODYEAR BRIDGESTONE

BRITISH MOBILE PENNZOIL

PERMANENT DISPOSABLE

PENS OIL

VAPE BOWLING

GREEN GOALING

REFORM...

U-TURN VACCINES

PATENT THOUGHTS,

NOTION ASSUMPTION,

PROPER PROPERTY LICENSE,

LINING OF THINKING, CERTIFICATE,

JOTTING ALONG CONCEPTUALIZING,

FREEDOM & LIBERTY

PERCEPTION PRESCRIPTION, SCRIPTURES,

JACOB & JEREMIAH'S JOBS

PATHS INDEED CAREERS

JOURNEY ENDS HERE,

ASSOCIATES...

FACE OF A BILL

SCORES SCORNS DOES IT,

NON-PROFIT ORGANIZATIONS,

TORTUOUS MOURN, STOP FUZZIN',

PEACEFUL PROTEST NUANCE,

MEDIA WAVES? CHESS MOVES?

MARS CAMS UFO ROVERS,

WE GOT MOVEMENT,

ON OUR TARGETS,

MARKED THE HALLS,

FOR SUGAR WARHEADS,

SLAVERY SALVATION UNCONSTITUTIONAL,

VIOLATION ON NINE, ELEVEN, & THIRTEEN,

AWFUL HOME COOKING,

TRESPASSING TREASURY,

RESERVED A RIGHT,

DO YOU & I,

FACE OUR ACCUSER?

STARING INTO MONEY...

TUNNEL VISIONS

OPTICAL ILLUSION,

IMAGERY FABRICATION,

LOGICAL & RATIONALIZATION,

CONCLUSION TO THE HYPOTHESIS,

SHALL OPEN NUMEROUS,

WINDOWS & DOORS TO,

OPPORTUNITIES, ALBEIT,

A PRUDENCE PRESENCE,

SETTLES IN...

CRISIS OF 116TH

SORRY SORROWS,

WORRY SPARROWS,

PARDON PARSON,

SKY PILOT,

SPACE CADET,

HOLY JOE,

SIP YOUR CUP OF JOE,

G.I. JOE, JOE DIRT,

PRESIDENT JOE MAMA,

A CURE???

A CLERIC???

AN ATTIRE???

CARREY A LIAR???

POPPY'S SEED, SESAME STREET,

A SALTY STAR,

EVERYTHING BAGEL,

LOX & NOVA,

BE ON ONE'S PAR...

ANSWERING MACHINE

STOLEN GUIDANCE,

BYLLAMING THE PAST,

INSTEAD OF CURRENT WAVES,

BROTHERLY SISTERLY LOVE,

DISTANCE RELATIONSHIP,

IS IT OUR BREAK-UP?

ARE WE GONNA MAKE UP?

CALL YOU LATER?

CHECKING ON YA,

JUST TO SAY SUP?

YOU ALIVE?

CALL BACK, PLEASE!!!

LOVE YA, SINCERELY,

HELL-O-O JEEZ-Z-Z!!!

S-S-SO-ORR-R-Y-Y,

FINE, ITS' POINTLESS...

SOMETIMES

SOMETIMES I FEEL,

AS IF,

I AM THE WHOLE TREASURY,

SOMETIMES I FEEL,

AS IF,

I AM TWO WASHINGTONS,

SOMETIMES I FEEL,

THE NEED

TO QUESTION LIFE,

SOMETIMES I FEEL,

THE NEED,

TO SEARCH FOR ANSWERS,

SOMETIMES I FEEL,

HOW & WHO,

I MAY BECAME,

SOMETIMES I FEEL,

WHAT & WHY,

I AM BECOMING...

SCENTS OF BREATH

ENCHANTING LIPS

SEAL A KISS

MISATOE, SECRET GARDEN,

WILTING ROSE,

MELATONIN HINTS,

MENTOS WINTER FRESH

TIC TAC, BAZOOKA,

DOUBLE MINT

PENNSYLVANIA & DELAWARE

RED HOT JUICY FRUIT...

HALLUCINATIONS

AMBIGUOUS ANTICIPATIONS IN CONTEMPT,

DETERMINE DESIRES, HIGHS, & LOWS,

DISTRAUGHT & POISED,

INFAMOUS REBUTTALS & CONTRADICTION

CONDEMNED, GOVERNED BY

TRANS FIXATION OF ALTER EFFECTS,

STATES OF THE MIND...

CARDINAL'S CARDIO

HEARTSTOPPER, DREAMBOAT,

HEART THROBBER, LEMON DROP,

TURTLE DOVE, DOODLE BUG,

YOU'RE THE NUCLEUS,

VIVACITY OF MY SOUL,

YOUR THE CORE; THE HUB,

MY HEART MY CITY OF GOLD...

OUR WORLD

TAXED & TESTED,

HARASSED & ARRESTED

CONSTRAINED TO CONFINEMENT

RESTRAINING THE VIOLENCE

SILENCE THEIR FEARS

PUPILS EYELIDS OF TEARS

DRY THE SHYS

MY GIRL; O' SIR,

MY BOY, MY DEAR,

OUR WORLD I HEAR

AS COMMANDERS PEERS CHEERS

POLITICAL CORRUPTION...

HOURS OF OUR GRAVES

FUNERAL PLOTS LIVING WILLS,

USUALLY PLOTS OF LIVING WELL,

WHAT IT DO?

ITS LIVING HELL,

PRONE BY THE STRESS,

STONE TO DEATH,

VEGETATION SIMULATES,

SHIPPING CHARGES & HANDLING,

FOR DELIVERANCE,

RID OF IGNORANCE,

CITY IN MORTISE

JIMMY HENDRIX & JIM MORRIS

1-800-FLOWERS

NUMBER TO THE FLORIST...

AN OPEN GATE

PROPAGATE,

A PROPERLY WAY,

TO OPEN ARRAY?

IS TO PROSCRIBE,

A UNITED WAY?

TO GIVE,

TO TAKE AWAY,

A UNIVERSAL PRAY?

TO LIVE,

TO STAY SAVE,

TO STAY SAFE?

CARBON FOOT

BABY CAN YOU BREATHE?

INHALE?! EXHALE?!

I GOT THIS FROM JAMAICA,

IT ALWAYS WORKS FOR ME,

DAKOTA TO DECATUR; UH HUH?

NO MORE PRETENDING,

UH, UH?

HEY, HEY, HEY,

NOW, NOW, CHIN UP,

HEY, HEY, HEY,

YOU'RE THE NEW BEGINNING,

BABY'S MY CONSEQUENCES,

MY KIND OF,

TRUTH OR DARE?

GAY BLISSFUL STARE...

OUT OF TOWN

HEY, BABY...

WHERE DO YOU COME FROM?

WELL SHE LOOKED AT ME & SMILED,

AND LOOKED AS IN DEEP THOUGHT,

GLANCING INTO SPACE...

"I'M COME FROM THE LAND WHERE,

NORTH RISES THE SUN."

THEN I SAID, "HEY BABY,

WHERE YA TRYIN' TO GO TO?"

SHE REPLIED,

"MANA, STAR OF THREE MOONS,"

PEACE OF MIND...

"DO YOU NEED A SQUIRE?"

"EVOLUTION IS ALL WE NEED,"

GRIN ACROSS,

HER TALKING LIPS,

PRESENTED HER CONVICTION,

A SADISTIC PHENOMENAL....

THEY LOVE

THEY LOVE,

OUR HEAVENLY BLESSINGS,

THEY LOVE,

OUR DEVILISH SIN,

THEY LOVE,

OUR CITY YIELDING BEYOND,

GOLD, SILVER, & RUPEES,

THEY LOVE,

OUR NURSERY STORY DEN,

SWEET DREAMS & GOOD NIGHTS

THEY LOVE,

OUR FORGIVING NATURE

THEY LOVE,

HOW WE ACCEPT THEM?

AND THEY US!!!

POETICALLY CHARGED

MY LOVES A FELONY,

I'M ADDICTED TO THE INK,

MY HEART'S A MELODY,

THE RHYTHMS THE BEAT,

THE DIAGNOSIS IS A MURMUR,

THE VISIONS THEY SEEK,

THE HYPNOSIS IS VERBAL,

DECIMALS OF DECIBELS,

AT IT NEGATIVE,

AND POSITIVE PEAKS,

REWIND BACK & PLAY

POETICALLY CHARGED...

SIDE OF THE ROAD

BLOWN CASKET & TIE RODS

URNS MONTESSORI,

FALSE PROPHECY,

MOUNTAIN OF GLORY,

STRESS NUMBER ONE,

COVID-19 BLURRY,

IMAGES ILLUSION

AUTHOR ILLUSTRATED,

MISSING ADMINISTRATION,

MIDDLE OF FRUSTRATION,

INCOMPETENCE ROTATION,

DELICATELY FED, SPOON BENT,

PLASTIC RATHER, STERLING UTENSILS,

TENSIONS ON PENSION,

IDEAL RETIREMENT DEPLETED,

EIGHT, NINE DEPRIVED,

IS THE BALCONY

TIER DECEASE?

DO I REST MY CASE?

PRICELESS VOYAGE

LOVE WORTH,

A 1000 PIRATE TREASURES, TREASURES,

AND I KNOW THE DEEP BLUE SEA,

I SWAM A 1000 MILES,

JUST TO FIND YOU,

I'VE BEEN LOST,

IN THE WAVES NOW,

THAT GOT PLAYED OUT,

AND IT CAME DOWN,

IT WAS CRASHING, CRASHING ON US,

CRASHING DOWN, DOWN, DOWN, DOWN,

A SHIPWRECK FULL OF GHOSTS?

CAPTAIN'S SKIPPER WASHED,

BY A DOLPHIN CAUCUS, ASHORE,

CREW PADDLING THE ROW,

RECOVERING THE RUM,

JEWS & GOLD,

YET ALL OF IT,

VANISHING AT DAWN...

IS THIS LOVE? IS THIS LUST?

HONEY, YOU'RE LIKE A DRUG,

I CAN'T GET ENOUGH,

IS THIS LOVE?, IS THIS LUST?,

ADDICTED, TO, YOUR TOUCH, (TOUCH)

HONEY, YOU'RE LIKE A DRUG,

I CAN'T GET ENOUGH,

IS THIS LOVE?, IS THIS LUST?,

FIENDING, FOR, YOUR LOVE, (LOVE)

BABY YOU'RE DA RUSH,

HONEY IS DA ITCH,

BABY YOU'RE MY VISE,

HONEY IS MY FIX,

GOT MY STOMACH IN KNOTS,

PUT MY BODY IN A TWITCH,

PLACE MY MIND IN A BIND,

YOUR ALL I THINK

WITHOUT MY DAILY DOSE

I TURN ILL

UNTIL YOU APPEAR...

HONEY, YOU'RE LIKE A DRUG,

I CAN'T GET ENOUGH,

IS THIS LOVE?, IS THIS LUST?,

ADDICTED, TO, YOUR TOUCH, (TOUCH)

HONEY, YOU'RE LIKE A DRUG,

I CAN'T GET ENOUGH,

IS THIS LOVE?, IS THIS LUST?,

FIENDING, FOR, YOUR LOVE, (LOVE)

YOU'RE THE FIX,

THE LIGHTER BOILING

CONTENT IN THE SPOON

THE PRICK, THE DRAWBACK,

SUBSTANCE ENTERING THE VEINS,

MISSING A DAY

I END UP DOPE SICK,

GOT ME HOPELESS,-LY,

UNDER YOUR SPELL,

EXPLODING THE CELL,

YOUR MY DOPE DEALER,

HOOK ME UP

IT'S YOUR ECSTASY THAT I WANT,

IT'S YOUR AFFECTION THAT I NEED,

A PARTNER IN CRIME

A FRIEND FOREVER MINE...

PAGES OF DECADES

PONDERING SORROWS,

ROTATION DWELLING,

SPHERES OF AN ATOM,

SPIRITUAL HELLIONS,

STARS' ESSENCES,

GLITTERS OF GRACE,

OH! FAITH; BELIEF BLINDED,

BY RAY, BANS,

TINTED FILM VISION,

OF ARTIFICIAL FILLERS,

OF HUMANITY'S EXTINCTION...

STAY & WAIT

STAY, STAY, STAY,

WAIT, WAIT, WAIT,

STAY FRIENDS,

STAY TIL IT ENDS,

STAY TIL IT BEGAN,

STAY TIL IT MENDS,

STAY, STAY, STAY,

WAIT, WAIT, WAIT,

STAY, STAY, STAY,

WAIT, WAIT, WAIT,

WAIT FRIENDS,

WAIT FOR ME,

WAIT FOR THEM,

WAIT FOR US,

STAY, STAY, STAY,

WAIT, WAIT, WAIT,

STAY, STAY, STAY,

WAIT, WAIT, WAIT...

DAUNTING MOURNING

DAUNTING MOURNING,

OF HAUNTING NIGHTS & MORNINGS,

IS PRAISE NOR TEMPT?

CONSCIENCE SNORING,

OF CONSTANT LIFE DRAWING,

AM I CAGED IN BED?

NOT NONSENSE ADORING,

A COMET STORMING,

IS IT FACE-OFF?

YET ASCEND GLORY,

CONFIDENT & WARMING,

ARE YOU ALARM?

FIRST CHESS MOVES

HEAD OF ROSE THORN

THORNE'S COUNSEL

THE ECLIPSE PANEL,

CROWN ROYAL,

BY NOBLEMEN TRIALS,

COURAGE & PATIENCE DISPLAYED,

OF A LUSTFUL WRATH,

AND PRIDEFUL ACCEPTANCE,

DISCIPLINE BY SELFISH GREED,

RATHER SHARED ENVY,

AMONGST BISHOPS & KNIGHTS,

ONLY PAWNS ARE FORTHCOMING,

ONLY ATTACKS; DIAGONAL,

FROM A BRANCH,

LEFT OR RIGHT???

BOTH IDENTICAL COLORS,

YET, ONE BLACK,

YET, ONE WHITE...

A TASTE

LINGERING TASTE,

OH! LONG THE TASTE,

NUMB TASTE, COINBASE,

A POINT; STAY SAFE,

STOLEN BASE,

SACRIFICE BUNT,

ELECTION HUNT,

DUCKS & PIGEON SEEDS,

BUCKET LIST NEEDS,

LOCKET KISS SINCERE,

YOUR CHOICE,

YOUR VOICE...

P.S.

SIGH OF RELIEF...

JOB APPLICATION

STIRRING AGGRAVATION,

ONLY STRESS PRONE,

ONE LOVE,

ONE ETERNALLY,

A DIVERSE DEMOGRAPHIC,

A UNIVERSE'S MEMO; GRASP IT,

PETRIFIED TO BE ANYTHING,

OTHER THAN A COLOR SIR,

PINK AND PURPLE DREAM,

CODEINE BLACK SYRUP,

HAVE MY AMERICAN PEOPLE?

LIVING LIVID; LUCID DREAM,

ABOVE THE INFLUENCE,

SUPPORTS DILUTED; NEED-A,

APPLY WITHIN...

IN WITH

IN HARMONY WITH

IN ORDINANCE WITH

IN ACCORDANCE WITH

ACCORDING TO THIS

ACCORDING WITH THIS

IN COMPUTE WITH

IN CONGRUENT WITH

IN COMMENSURATE WITH

APPROPRIATE & BEFITTING

SURELY BEFITTING,

GOOD RIDDANCE!!!

CYBERSEX

PUNDIT AS A GENIUS

MASTER, A PROFESSIONAL,

MAVEN HOTSHOT WHIZ,

ACE SAVANT

SCHOLAR FOR INTELLECT

MAHARISHI SOLOMON

ALLEVIATE,

A DANGEROUS PATE

A DANGEROUS FATE

SHE MUST BE

BLOGGING MY GRAVE

LOG IN; PASSWORDS,

SOD DOS

CHARLIE HOLD SHIFT

SEMI-COLON

SIDE SLASH,

SIDE SLASH,

ALPHA BETA DELTA

ECHO & GIGAS...

STAGES OF SUCCESS

FERVID & ARDENT LOVE,

A STATE OF INEBRIATION,

STEERING WHILE IMPAIRED,

JEERING SNEERING STARES,

MENTAL STAIRS & LADDERS,

VINES DRAPE WHISPERS,

A SIGN DEEP POSTED,

CLIMB & BEWARE,

MAGNETS RESIDE ABOVE,

CLASHING ZONE,

DIM ALLURE APPEARS,

THROUGH THE CLOUDS

DARE DO ENTER..

CURRENCY TRIP

ROAD TO A PENNY

ROUTE TO A NICKLE

COMMUTE TO A DIME,

TOURING A QUARTER,

JOURNEY & A HALF,

DESTINY TO A DOLLAR

EXPLORING A WASHINGTON,

PATHS OF HONEST ABE,

LANES TO HAMILTON,

FREEWAYS TO JACKSON

TRAILS OF GRANTS

STREETS OF FRANKLIN...

KEEP OFF THE ROCKS

KEEP OFF THE ROCKS,

THOSE LAVA ROCKS, TURN HOT?

COALS OR METAMORPHIC ROCKS,

THAT'S THAT GATOR, THAT'S THAT DROP,

DIFFERENT PLAYAS, DIFFERENT BLOCKS,

DIFFERENT LAYERS? SEDIMENTARY ROCKS

FLINTSTONE SPARKS, SAFETY PEBBLES,

CINDERBLOCK, KEY LIME & MARBLE

SWORD IN THE STONE, KING AUTHOR

CORAL REEF AERIAL & LOBSTER,

KEEP OFF THE ROCKS

THOSE LAVA ROCKS, TURN HOT?

ARE YOU STANDING,

ON THAT?

COST OF LOVE

COST OF LOVE,

A SILVER'S VALUE?

IS EQUAL TO GOLD?

THE HEART IT'S FROM,

IS THE APPRAISAL.

COST OF LOVE ,

A SILVER'S PRICE?

IS SAME TO GOLD?

THE SENTIMENT IT'S FROM,

IS THE INDIVIDUAL.

COST OF LOVE,

A SLITHER OF TIME?

A HELLO; A GOODBYE?

YOU WELL; YOU ALIVE?

COST OF LOVE,

ENDLESS & EVERLASTING...

OLD THEM

OLD I

OLD THEM

OLD ISLAND

O-O-O-RI-ON,

O-O-O-RI-ON,

OVER IVAN

ORDER HAWAIIAN

ORDER WISE MEN

ORDER ITEMS, &

OR, OR, OR,

VITA-MINS,

ORB VITALS &,

OR, ORGANS, OREGON,

ORES & GEMS

OLD THEM

OLD I, AGAIN...

UNANSWERED

ARE, WARS EMERGING?

ARE, FAITH DIMINISH?

ARE, ART NOT FACTS?

ARE, SCIENCE NOT FICTION?

ARE, CONCLUSIONS ENDINGS?

ARE, ILLUSIONS INTENTIONAL?

ARE, FEELING MUTUAL?

ARE, BONDS TIES?

ARE, HAPPY EVER AFTERS' HAPPY?

ARE, HERO'S LOSERS?

ARE, VILLAINS' WINNERS?

SCREENPLAY

NOTICE ME, YET,

HOPELESS SUSPENSE

ROMANTIC RIDDANCE

ONE OF THOSE LOVE STORIES

LOVE SONG, LOVE NOTE,

COUPLE TICKETS

ADMISSION, ADMISSION,

SELF-CENTERED CHILDREN

DRAMA WORTH

NARROW MINDED TEENAGE STARS

INTERMISSION

PLAY WORTH

RENOVATION ADULTS & SENIORS

INTERMISSION

SCRIPT WORTH

VOICE & VOCALS...

I'M CAGED IN

I'M CAGED IN,

THEY WON'T LET ME OUT,

THEIR AFRIAD THAT,

MY DEVILS & DEMONS

MAY COME OUT...

I'M CAGED IN,

THEY WON'T LET ME OUT,

THEIR AFRAID THAT

MY GHOST & GHOULS,

MAY COME OUT...

I GOT THEM SCARRED,

I GOT THEM NERVOUS,

I GOT THEM IN CHURCH

I GOT THEM IN SERVICE

TEMPLE ON FRIDAY

MONDAY IN COURT

PLEADING TIL TUESDAY

DREADING A WEDNESDAY'S DIVROVCE

AS THRUSDAY WORRIES

APPROACH!

I'M CAGED IN,

THEY WON'T LET ME OUT,

THEIR AFRIAD THAT,

MY DEVILS & DEMONS

MAY COME OUT...

I'M CAGED IN,

THEY WON'T LET ME OUT,

THEIR AFRAID THAT

MY GHOST & GHOULS,

MAY COME OUT...

I HAVE THEIR INSERCUITIES

I HAVE THEM AS I MAY

I HAVE THEIR SINS

I HAVE THEM AS PREY

I HAVE THEIR HORRORS

I HAVE THEM ALL EYES

I HAVE THEIR NIGHTMARES

I HAVE THEM AS I...

I'M CAGED IN,

THEY WON'T LET ME OUT,

THEIR AFRIAD THAT,

MY DEVILS & DEMONS

MAY COME OUT...

I'M CAGED IN,

THEY WON'T LET ME OUT,

THEIR AFRAID THAT

MY GHOST & GHOULS, MAY COME OUT...

SURFING THE WEB

SOLID WHITE

ALBACORE TUNA

IN WATER

NET DRAINED

OF CHARCTERS

A BOARD OF KEYS

OMEGA-3S

CAPS TABS

SHIFT CONTROL

ALTERNATE STAR

FIGURES EIGHTS,

AIRPLANE MODE

MILEHIGH CLUB

ALIENATED FROM HOME

ALIENATED FROM HOME

GRAVITY PLUNDERS

FLASH DROWNING,

INSIDE ERUPTIONS

OUTBURSTS STEEMING

VOICE QUAKES

LIKE A TRYANTS TOUNGE,

DEFYING THEIR OWN DICTATION,

PRESUCATION & EXCUTION

LOST FOR WORDS

LOST FOR WORDS

LOST OF THOUGHTS

LOST WITHOUT YOU

BY MY SIDE

CAN YOU BE

MY REMINDER

OFF COURSE

RUNNING IN CIRCLES

WHEN VANISHED

CAN YOU BE

MY FORMER

YET DIFFERENT

IN EACH ANGLE

RARE & AUTHENTIC

DOWN TO EARTH

GENUINE & SINCERE

CAN YOU BE

MY GRIP OF REALITY

MY LOVE AFFAIR

WITH IMPERFECTION

FIXING US

BY FIXING ME

ANY ADVICE

IM ALL EARS

CAN YOU BE

MY CONFESSION

MY INVESTMENT

MY ETERNITY

MY BEST FRIENDS

IS THE STACKS

TOO LOW?

IS THE RISK

TOO HIGH?

IS THE CASE

TOO SHORT?

IS THE SENTENCE

TOO LONG?

LOST FOR WORDS

LOST THOUGHTS

LOST WITHOUT YOU

BY MY SIDE

CAN YOU BE

MY SANITY

MY SANCTURARY

MY MEDICATION

CAN YOU BE

MY MAGICIAN

MY FANTASY

MY MEDITATION

CAN YOU BE

MY ANSWER

WHEN I DON'T

HAVE A CLUE

PUZZLED SCRABBLE

UPWORD TEAMMATES

WHEN IM IN A STRUGGLE

WHEN IM IN TROUBLE

WHEN I JUST NEED A HUG

WHEN I JUST WANNA SNUGGLY

LOST FOR WORDS

LOST THOUGHT

LOST FOR THOUGHT

LOST WITHOUT YOU

BY MY SIDE

CAN YOU BE

MY PARTNER IN CRIME

MY GARDEN I PRESENT

MY DANDY LION

CAN YOU BE

MY HAND ME DOWN

MY SOUP KITCHEN

MY ARMY OF SALVATION

CAN YOU BE

MY PUSH MY TUG

MY PULL MY NUDGE

MY AMBITION

MY MOTIVATION

ARE YOU ABLE

TO BE MY SMILE

ARE YOU ABLE

TO BE MY TRIAL

ARE YOU ABLE

TO BE MY BILE

ARE YOU ABLE

TO BE MY FIRE

LOST FOR WORDS

LOST FOR THOUGHT

LOST WITHOUT YOU

BY MY SIDE

DEAD VIRUS

PSYCHOLOGY PSYCHICS

RABIES SHOTS

DISEASE WARFARE

JESUS OH MAN

REMEDY WORKING EFFICIENT.

VIRUS'S DYING

VIRUS'S DEMISE

VIRUS'S DEATH

VIRUS'S DEAD

CURE AFFECTIVE...

PRICELESS ORDER

CLOCK OF SCALE

TRIPLE OR DIGITAL

LIBERTY OF CORRUPT

ENSLAVED JUSTICE

GRAVEL OAKS

WHITTLED BY A CRAVER

A CLOTH OF HONOR

A COAT OF INTERIGTY

A CODE OF SEALS

A COACH OF DISPLINE

A COURT OF LAW

A CORE OF FLAWS

ACORN, SUPREME DOORS...

APHRODISIAC

EXQUISITE SAVOR

APPETITE & STOMACHED

TASTE BUD & AROMAS

PALATES BETWEEN

THE ROOF OF THE MOUTH,

SALIVA DROOLING

AND THE NASAL CAVITY,

DEEP INHALE

OF THE DESIRE TANGY

INGREDIENTS

A RECIPE OF PLEASURE

SERVED & READY

A SWEET DESERT

PRAY NO. 1

PRAYING FOR OTHERS

FORGIVENESS

IS IT A SIN?

IS IT NOBLE?

PRAYING FOR OTHERS

UNDERSTANDING

IS IT A GIFT?

IS IT A CURSE?

NO ANSWER.

NO RESULTS.

AIN'T IT THOU

ANTIDOTE

ANTIDOTE

ANSWER A POET

ILLUSION CONCLUSION

RESOLUTIONS SOLUTIONS

AROUND THE WORLD

SCHOOL, HORSE, WHISTLE BLOWER,

BLACK BEAUTY & MISTER ED

NIGHT NICK BOOKING NOVELS

FOR RENT, FOR ELECTRIC

FOR WATER FOR LIVING

ANTIDOTE, ANTIDOTE

AIN'T IT THOU

ANCIENTS MOAN

SCHOOL SUPPLIES

OUTLINES TRACING

PENCILED IN LEAD

NO. 2, PREFERABLY

PAPER LOOSE LEAF

MEAD COLLEGE RULED

PEN MATE BLUE INK

YELLOW SHARPIE HIGHLIGHTS

SPECIFIC PROJECTOR NOTES

WRITTEN IN THE DARK

COURSE SYLLABUS

AND SCHOOL SUPPLIES

PROHIBITION

GIMME SUM, BUBBLEGUM,

DAT SOUR DOUGH, DAT SOUR D,

FILL A BOWL OF FRUITY PEBBLES,

BREAKFAST WITH DA GREEN QUEEN,

LUCKY CHARMS AND APPLE JACKS ,

AN EIGHTH OF DA GREEN BEEM,

AN EIGHTH OF DA BLUE GRASS ,

A QUARTER OF DAT BLUE DREAM,

AND AN OUNCE, OF DAT GREEN CRACK,

MR. WEED MAN,

I'M SEARCHING FOR MY ISLAND GIRL, MY CINDERELLA,

MY JULIET, MY LA LYBELLA,

MY DREAM QUEEN , MY WONDER WOMAN,

MY SUGAR BABY, MY SUGAR PLUM,

MY MAGIC CARPET RIDE, WITH JASMIN

COMPASS POLARS

SHE WAS ERRATIC

DARING & UNPREDICTABLE,

SPONTANEOUS & BLUNT,

AT TIMES, DEVIOUS & EVASIVE,

STILL, HONEST & LOYAL,

FAR FROM PERFECT,

YET, UN-PARALLEL,

DEVOTED TO HER

CORDIAL PASSION,

OF A TRUE SINCERE,

GENUINE LOVE,

HE WAS EAGER TO BE COMMITTED,

DEDICATED TO HER INSECURITIES AND QUERIES,

OF HESITATION BY AMBIVALENCE

OF OTHERS EQUIVOCATION.

BEYOND THE GRAVE

PROFUSELY HER SOLICITUDE,

AN AFFECTION TOWARDS,

HIS REVAMP TRANSMOGRIFIED

EMINENCE WAS HEROIC

GLORIFIED; BY SIMULTANEOUSLY,

ENCHANTING HER VOICE,

AS IT DAWDLES,

LINGERING IN THE WIND,

SURMISING YOU ARE,

MY FINAL DECIDER,

THE ONE I LONG,

TO BE WITH,

SACREDLY CLOSE

ARE YOU AFRAID?

OF THE DARK

AT MID-NIGHT?

ARE YOU BLINDED?

BY THE RAYS

OF THE LIGHT?

SACREDLY CLOSE,

COMFORTABLE NUMB,

TWO DIVINE SPIRITS

INTERTWINED BY HEART,

ARE YOU AFRAID

OF THE DARK

AT MIDNIGHT?

ARE YOU BLINDED

BY THE RAYS

OF THE LIGHT?

SACERDLY CLOSE,

COMFORTABLE NUMB,

DIVINE SPIRITS,

LOVING OUR SOULS

POODLES & PUGS

CHEATED CHEETAH,

DEFRAUD THE FROG

MISLEAD THE TOAD

BY SWINDLING FLIES

DECEIVED & DOUBLE CROSSED

THE TADPOLES DISLOYAL

UNFAITHFUL, LETDOWN

POSSES PLAY FALSE

TWO-TIME BLUFFING RAT

WEASLE DONE ME DIRTY

SOLD ME DOWNRIVER

TO THE PIGS, SNAKES,

AT ROTTWEILER JAILHOUSE

POODLE & PUGS

JUDGE BLACK WIDOW

NAME TAGS

ARE YOU LOSING IT?

WHILE SEARCHING

&

FINDING YOURSELF

MIGHT'VE LOST IT?

NOPE

STILL ON TRACK

STILL ON COURSE

IS YOUR MIND

ALERT & FUNCTIONAL

MAYBE A TAD OFF

IS THIS BRAIN

YOURS OR MINES

HELLO PSYCHO

I'M SOCIOPATH

ANSWER THE QUESTION

ONE MORE TIME

I WANT CONTROL

THUG MUSIC

THE MOVEMENT

WILL SOOTH THE SOUL

MAKE YOU LOSE CONTROL

MAKE YOU CHEW YOUR SHIRTS

MAKE YOUR PHONE

CONVERSATION TO A MINIMAL

HUNGER NATION TOP CRIMINAL

THOUGHTS ORIGINAL, FROM

THE NEXT ONE

RESULTS TO PROTECTION

A SUPPLEMENT OF ADULTS

SHOWING DIRECTION

NO AFFECTION

OR LOVE VERB EMERGE

SECTION OFF

FOR THE THUGS

SERVING BIRDS

HAD THE NERVES

TO MURDER AN INDIVIDUAL

FOR VISUAL COMBATS

OF STREET COMBAT

BETWEEN RACKETS

RAGS, MAGS, BODY BAGS

FILMING GOTTI DRAGS

THE SHOTTIE ADDS

ANOTHER BROTHER'S SOUL

TO A PLACE UNKNOWN

THEY FACE ALONE

THEIR OWN TROUBLES

STAY OUT FOR DAYS

ENDURING THE STRUGGLE

COUPLE OF DUTCH MASTERS

HAS A DAD

YET THEIR FATHER FIGURE

INHOUSE PLASTERED

RATHER SIP THE LIQUOR

RATHER THAN ANSWER

LIKE YOU DON'T EXSINT

DON'T ENLIST

ON THEIR STANDARDS

NO MANNERS

TOWARD HUMANITY

DON'T IF A FUCK

IF THEIR MAD AT ME

THE INSANITY DROVE

THE PLAN TO LOADED

EXPLODE WITH NO MOTIVE

FOR ANY EVENT

MAKES PLENTY OF SENSE

TO THEM, IN A LIFE OF SIN,

BETTER THINK TWICE THEN

CONSEQUENCE OF A PRISM

A PRISON,

EYE FOR AN EYE

IMPOSSIBLE MISSION

CONSIDER THEM DRIVEN

LIVING THE WAY THEY PLEASE

TIL' THEIR ON

THEIR PRAYING KNEES

THAT'S THAT

THUG MUSIC

I AM ALL EARS

THAT'S THAT

THUG MUSIC

O' MAY DEAR

THAT'S THAT

THUG MUSIC

IT ENDS HERE

ME & US

ME & THE PIE IN THE SKY

US & A PRECIOUS LONE GEM

ME & THE CHOIR OF THE NIGHT

US & PESSIMIST OLD MAN

ME & THE TRIBES DRUMS

US & TOXIC SMOG

ME & A LIFE'S CRISIS

US & HAPPILY EVER AFTER

ME & I LIKE IT

US TOO

US TOO!!!

COMICAL

NOSTRIL-ING CARBON,

DOWN MY SPINE,

FUMES & CHILLS,

SPONTANEOUS INTERTWINE,

NURTURING REVENGE,

AVENGER OF MINE,

GENERATION OF STRUGGLES,

LONGER REIGN,

ON BOTH LANES

IS WHAT, WORTH?

IS WHAT YOU SEEK?

WORTH TO HIDE?

IS WHAT YOU FIND?

WORTH TO KEEP?

IS WHAT YOU REAP,

WORTH TO AMEND?

IS WHAT YOU DESCEND?

WORTH TO ASCEND?

NEW NURSERY TALES

OXYGEN AFFECTION

FROM THE STILLNESS

WATERING BLOSSOMED SEEDS

BEYOND ROOTS STAGES

INFANTS GERM-FREE,

URGENCY OF LIFE'S MYSTERIES

IMMUNITY

MESSAGE

MESSAGE IN A CANDLE

MESSAGE IN A FORGIVENESS

MESSAGE IN A SIN

MESSAGE IN A ERROR

MESSAGE IN A PRAY

MESSAGE IN AN INK,

MESSAGE IN A TEXT,

MESSAGE IN A BOTTLE,

MESSAGE IN A POST,

MESSAGE IN EMAIL,

MESSAGE IN A HASHTAG,

MESSAGE IN A BRAND,

MESSAGE IN A PICTURE,

MESSAGE IN A IMAGE,

MESSAGE IN A CLOUD,

MESSAGE IN A STAR,

MESSAGE IN A VOICE,

MESSAGE IN A EXPRESSION,

MESSAGE IN A EXPERIENCE,

MESSAGE IN A BOOK,

MESSAGE IN AN ARTICLE,

MESSAGE IN SCREENPLAY,

MESSAGE IN A MOVIE,

MESSAGE IN A SONG,

MESSAGE IN A POEM,

MESSAGE IN A QUOTE,

MESSAGE IN A SIGN,

MESSAGE IN A BODY,

MESSAGE IN A EMOTION,

MESSAGE IN A LANGUAGE,

MESSAGE IN ART,

MESSAGE IN SILENCE,

MESSAGE IN YOU,

A MESSAGE IN ME...

WORLD'S RODEO

HOVERING THE LAMINATE,

AS GRAVITY WAS

NON-EXISTENT

GLIDING THE STARS

IN A UNIVERSAL TWIRL

CAUTION OF YOUR

HANDS & FEET

DANGEROUS TWISTS

MAY OCCUR,

IN A SANDSPUR

HEEL ON THE STOOL

TENDER TWO...

PORCELAIN

PORCELAIN, PORCELAIN,

VOMITING MY CHOW,

PORCELAIN, PORCELAIN,

DIARRHEA & BOWELS,

PORCELAIN, PORCELAIN,

TOILET OF BODY FLUIDS

PORCELAIN, PORCELAIN,

SOIL, FOUL, AS A SEWER,

PORCELAIN, PORCELAIN,

MADE POSSIBLE TO CONSUME

PORCELAIN, PORCELAIN,

WHERE I EAT MY FOOD,

PORCELAIN, PORCELAIN,

WHERE THE DOGS?

DRINK & DROOL,

PORCELAIN, PORCELAIN,

THRONE OF DAILY NEWS,

PORCELAIN, PORCELAIN,

THE DRAIN FLUSHES,

UNOCCUPIED, NEXT TO USE...

DAD ONCE HIS SOCIAL SECURITY DISABILITY CLASS SETTLED

AFTER BEING DIAGNOSE WITH BI-POLAR SCHIZOPHRENIC.

LONG REHAB, SUBSTANCE ABUSE, AND COUNTLESS MENTAL

& EMOTIONAL, VERBAL, & AT TIMES PHYSICAL ABUSE & ALTERCATION.

SOON AFTER THINGS IN THE OUR FAMILIES LIFE SEEM TO GET BETTER..

MONTH BEFORE BEING PLACED IN AN INSTITUTION
FOR 2WEEKS TO 90DAYS. TIMES TIME 30DAYS.
NUMEROUS ACCOUNTS BEING HOSPITALIZED.

ABOUT AUTHOR

RODERICK A. WILLIAMS BORN IN LONG ISLAND, NEW YORK IN JULY 1984. CURRENTLY RESIDES IN DELRAY BEACH FLORIDA. HIS FRATERNAL GRANDPARENTS WERE AWARD CUSTODY AFTER ILLEGAL NARCOTICS, ALCOHOLIC, & PSYCHOLOGY ABUSIVE BECAME A DAILY ROUTINE BY HE WAS SIX. HIGH SCHOOL DROPPED OUT, LATER COLLEGE...VICTIM OF AMERICA'S OPPRESSION, STATUS QUO HARDSHIPS OF 90'S. FAMILY DIVIDED BY A BROKEN JUSTICE SYSTEM OF THE 21ST CENTURY, WAR ON TERROR, COVID-19, THE VARIES OF DRUG EPIDEMICS, CORRUPT GOVERNMENT, CYBER-ATTACKS, & PANDEMIC. EVEN WORSE TRUMP AS THE 45TH PRESIDENT. BEING SILENCED. UNHEARD! UNSPOKEN! INSPIRED HIM DURING TO WRITE THE BOOK, HIS FIRST PUBLISHED. SINCE BEFORE I WAS THIRTEEN, I'VE BEEN WRITING LITTLE ART PATTERN IN MY ADOLESCENCE ABOUT GOT INTO POEMS, QUOTES, ELDER SAYINGS. IN 2016, AFTER DECIDING TO COLLEGE AT ASHFORD UNIVERSITY, RESIDING IN DELRAY BEACHES AT THE TIME OF THE PARKLAND SCHOOL SHOOTING, I CHANGE MY DEGREE TO PSYCHOLOGY, SINCE SPRING OF 2018 I'VE BEEN ACADEMIC FAILURE, MY LAST TWO GENERAL COURSE FAILING.

SINCE, I BEGAN TO FREEWRITING MORE. DONATING TO EDUCATION, MENTAL, & HEALTH NON-PROFITS,

ONE OF STORIES, ABOUT BEING A VIETNAMESE SOLDIER (FALSE),

OR BEING ON THE NEW YORK / NEW JERSEY PORTS AS A SUPERVISIOR (TRUE).

STORIES VARIED. SO DID BEHAVIORS. SUBSTANCE ABUSE, DOMESTIC ABUSE,

COUNTIUNED TO ERMERGING & VANISH, AFTER MULTIPLE DOSAGE CHANGES.

www.ingramcontent.com/pod-product-compliance
Lightning Source LLC
Chambersburg PA
CBHW081519250726
48659CB00009B/2857